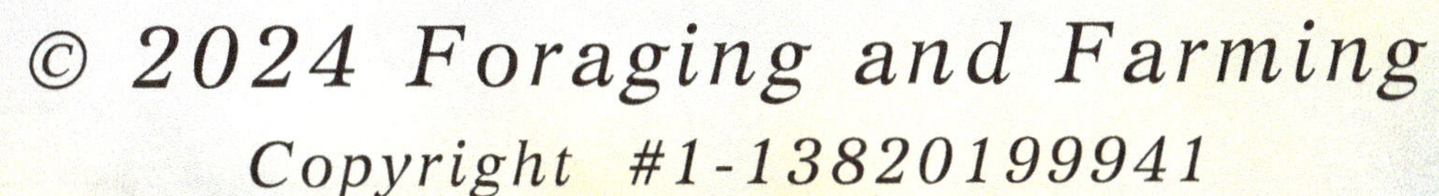

ABOUT

Food is a common thread that touches all aspects of our lives. I produce informative and engaging content about people doing extraordinary things for our food system.

This book is designed to be a resource for anyone exploring the basics of heirloom seeds, harvesting, seed saving, seed banks, and community-driven heirloom projects.

CONTENTS

CONTENTS

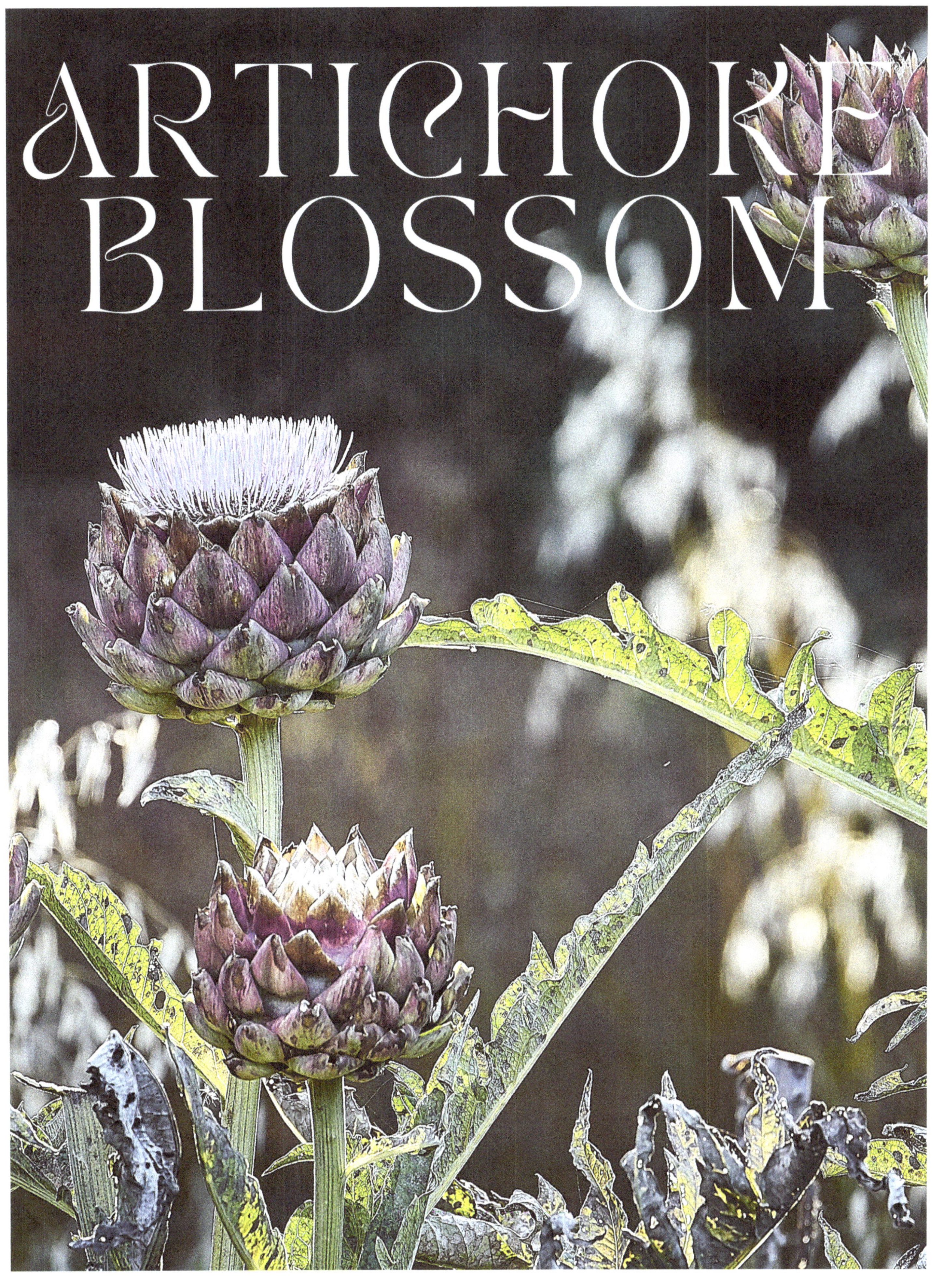
ARTICHOKE
BLOSSOM

introduction

An heirloom seed is the foundation of any family that keeps its story alive. Heirlooms describe the heritage and backstory being passed down from generation to generation. An heirloom varietal must be open-pollinated by birds or bees. Heirloom plants make up the holistic story of a family's agricultural history.

As I search the country for heirlooms to grow, I learn more about the stories embedded within our seed savers. It becomes more apparent that preserving these seeds is key to the stories that are embodied in us all. Seeds named – "Ketchup and Mustard," Tomatoes, and "Basil Genovese".

Food grown from heirloom seeds connects us through all types of experiences and brings us together when we gather for meals, share recipes, and laugh. Fondly, I recall walking our fields with my grandfather.

— WINTER SQUASH

On those surveys, he taught me about every aspect of fruits, vegetables, and herbs, some of which he might have made up along the way. But he knew how to grow food and raise meat for his family.

We grew Caraway seeds against the barns because they were not only a source for making soft Rye Bread, which we loved so much, but we also used them to prevent leaf hoppers and beetles from breeding.

There are remnants of heirloom Dahlias near our cold-spring-fed bog, just beyond the farm's back porch. Those seeds and tubers came from our Great-grandfather Heinrich.

My family handed down Heirlooms (seeds with a story) for us to embrace our heritage and history, as those stories became a Farm-to-Table heritage we carry in our hearts today. ■

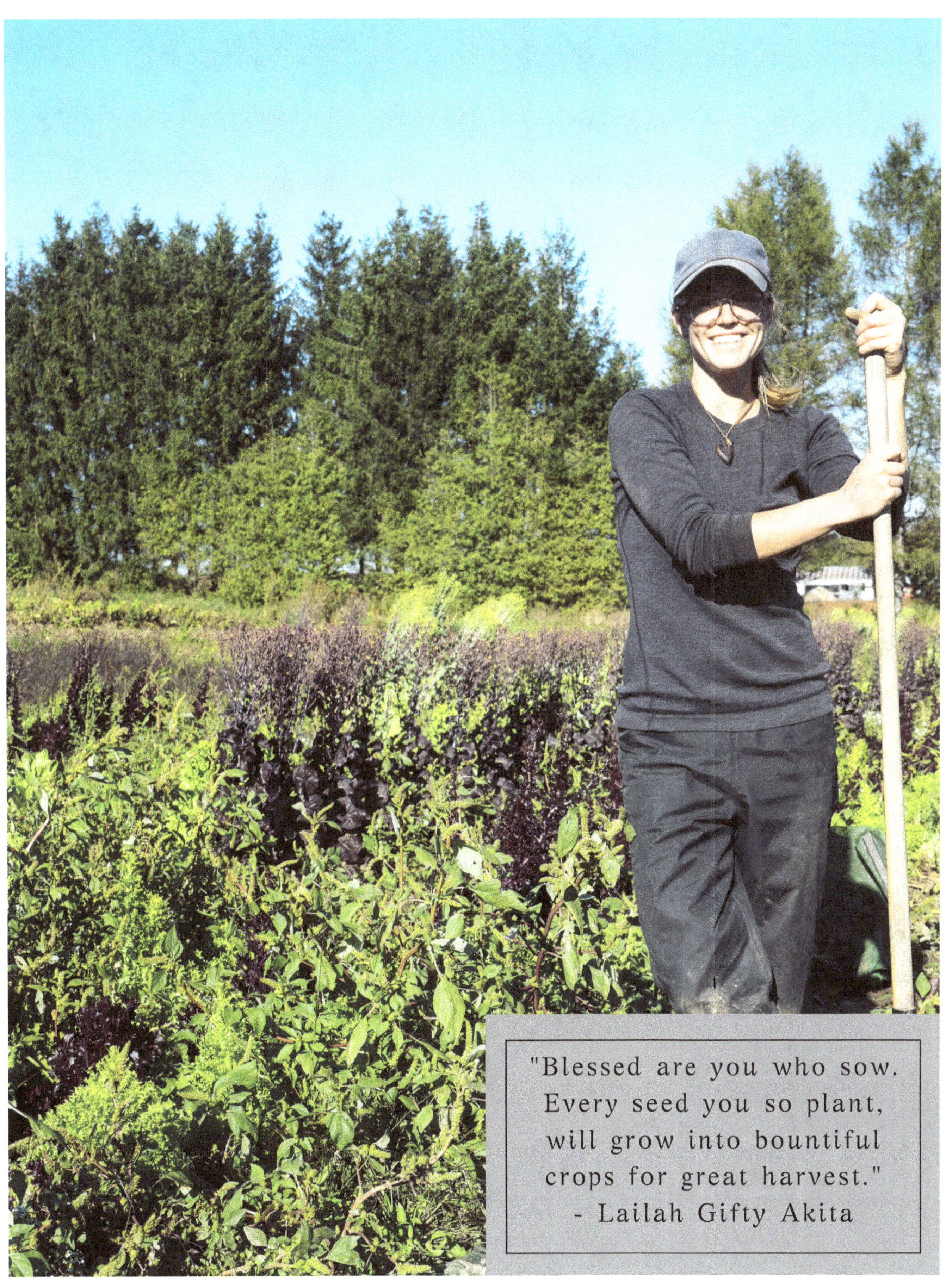

"Blessed are you who sow.
Every seed you so plant,
will grow into bountiful
crops for great harvest."
- Lailah Gifty Akita

HEIRLOOMS

definition of an heirloom

An heirloom, as it relates to plants and agriculture, is a seed, fifty years or older, saved from the plants of past harvest, stored and cataloged in a cool and dry place.

Heirloom describes the legacy or backstory being passed down from generation to generation. An heirloom varietal must be open-pollinated by birds or bees. Heirloom plants make up the holistic story of a country's agricultural history.

Heirlooms have a place in agriculture, bringing forth a unique and tasteful variety of non-mass-produced fruits and vegetables. They are non-genetically modified organisms (non-GMO); they can't be changed to adjust for taste, usability, or even uniformity.

Heirloom seeds bring the joy of planting, tending, and harvesting. Each variety's name, color, and shape give way to inspiration.

chard

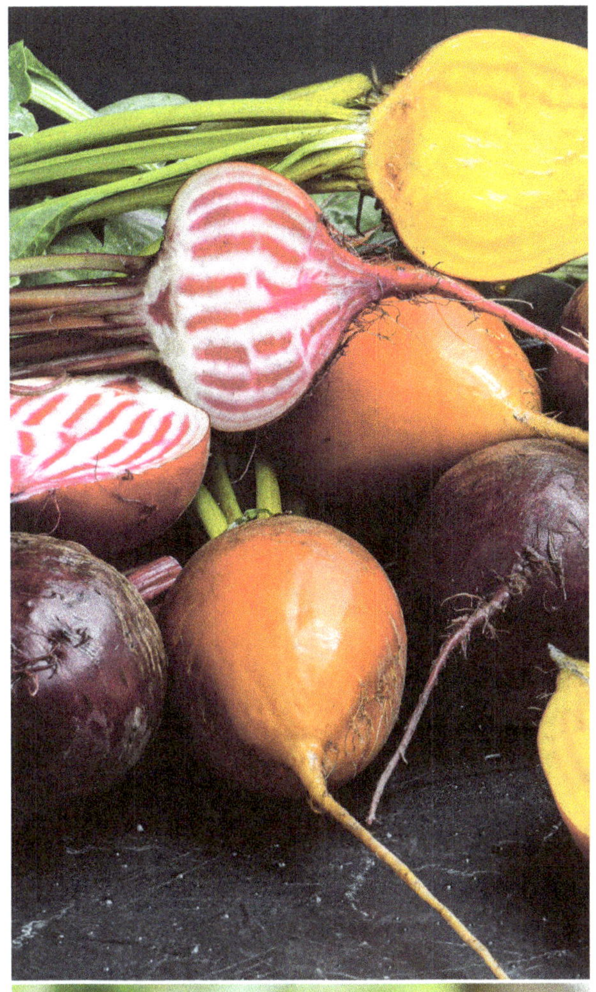

We've grown accustomed to seeing that perfect tomato fit to spec on our hamburger bun, while also avoiding those pesky, disfigured, or discolored vegetables at the market.

Some of us go to great lengths to change that summer squash with the brown marking as if we are getting cheated on that ounce of damaged product.

Heirloom seeds tend to have a variety of environmental sensitivities regarding planting, survival, and adversity to weather and soil conditions. Conventional farming is built around scale, speed, and consistency.

Harvesting good-tasting food for those Sunday suppers, selecting the right eggplant variety, lettuce, radish, and other vegetables, and "planning before you plant" are crucial.

Seeds are the history of a farmer's legacy, their story of pride and hard work. The output of their effort comes from the ability to share stories through food. ■

turnip

GLOBAL SEED BANK

I sit in my world, step back, and look at the universe as a whole; instead of compartmentalizing, I ask why. Even during a time of war, when people are at odds in places like Ukraine or Israel, people counterbalance those efforts by taking steps to save our agricultural history, otherwise known as the seed savers.

I can't help but think about the collaborative work going into saving the seeds of our food system. The Svalbard Global Seed Vault safeguards over 1.2 million seeds from over 70 countries, preserving crop research and plant science for humanity.

In October of 2023, the country of Ghana was Svalbard's 100th depositor of copies of seeds from generations past and quite possibly the future of our food system.

Writing an article on what some might say is an overwritten topic may be right, but if human nature prevails, a fluid conversation about the future of food and farming should be on our list.

Trending analytics and the focus on preserving the integrity of our food system. Some will ask why we haven't done better due diligence with tubers and food like bananas.

Maybe others are thinking about wild seed and preserving the grasses and woody mass; the truth is, we are taking action, but this whole process of building and supporting an all-inclusive time capsule takes a significant amount of time and human resources.

Perched along the hill between the Svalbard Satellite Station and the airport, etched into the landscape, is an illuminated structure built into the permafrost of the Arctic Circle.

Carved into the side of the hill, nearly 500 feet into the earth – the seed vault was architected by Peter Søderman, a concrete gray wedge, perfectly sculpted, able to house 4.5 million crop varieties, as noted by The Crop Trust.

The illuminescent structure, designed an implemented by Dyveke Sanne, was built with the symbology of a guiding light, named "Perpetual Repercussion". The Svalbard Global Seed Vault was established and is owned by the country of Norway.

It operates in a unique partnership between the Norwegian Ministry of Food and Agriculture, the regional gene bank NordGen, and The Crop Trust, an independent international organization supporting education and recordkeeping for the safeguarding of our seeds.

The online virtual tour is sponsored by three organizations: The Norwegian Ministry of Foreign Affairs, NordGen, and The Crop Trust, which are all participants and stewards of the seed vault.

The Ministry of Norway allows any gene bank interested in depositing seed copies to submit and catalog samples into the vault. The first step is to email seedvault@nordgen.org, requesting when you want to send seed copies to the facility.

For the adventurous at heart, there are a handful of ways to visit the [Svalbard Global Seed Vault](). The Global Seed Vault is closed to visitors, but you can participate in interactive hikes near the site through Svalbard Wildlife Expeditions and Longyearbyen, as well as 2-hour taxi tours. ∎

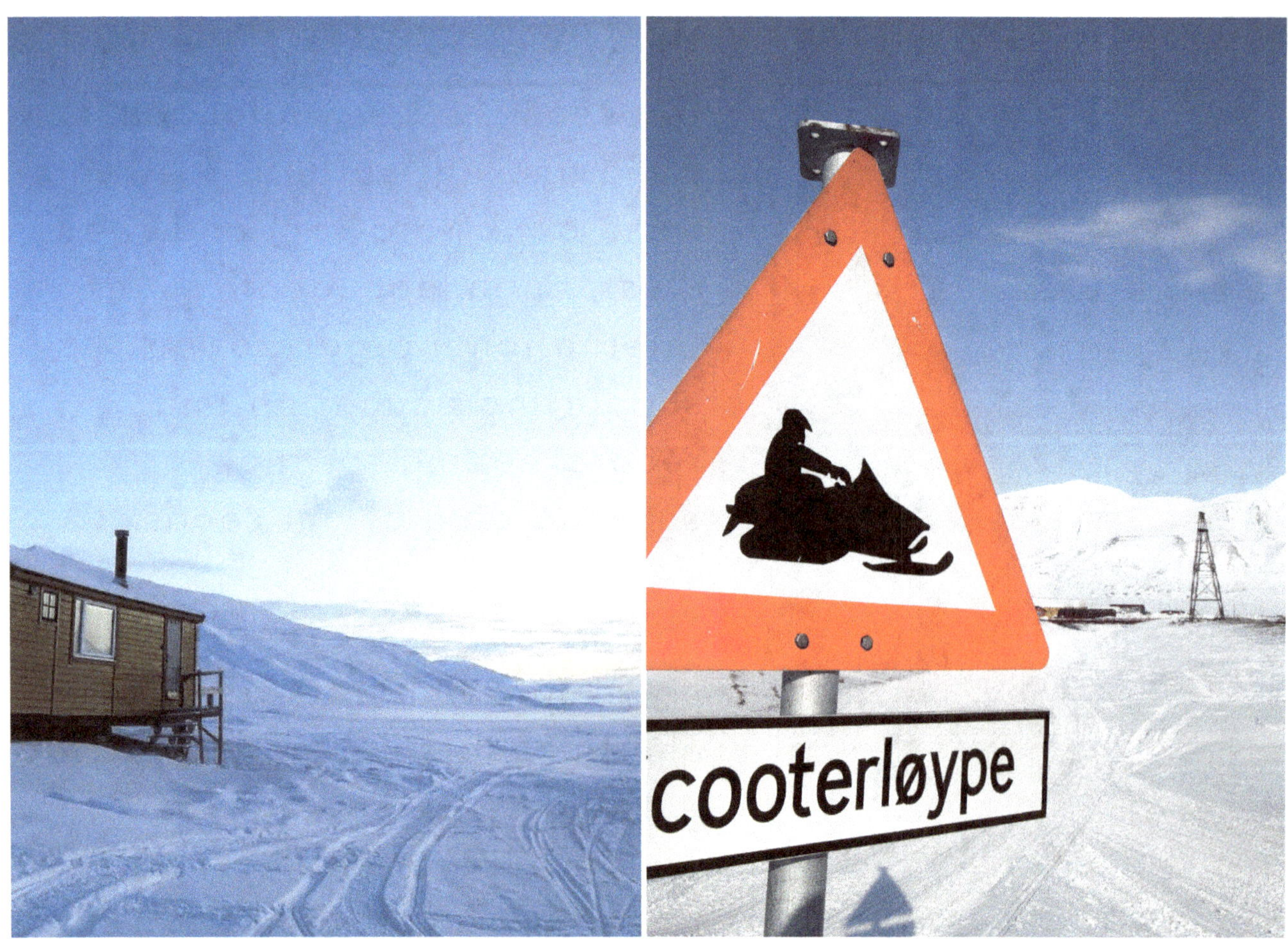

seed policy

Seed sharing is an age-old practice of increasing plant diversity. When it comes to seed policy and state laws, California is one of the only exempt entities regarding seed sharing.

Today, seed sharing is illegal in U.S. states such as Pennsylvania, Maryland, Minnesota, and Nebraska. We'll dig into the details later in the book, of course.

If seed sharing is not illegal in your state, it is important to apply for a permit and submit to testing requirements and other regulations to be empowered to store, share, or sell heirlooms and other heritage seeds - if you are looking to build a seed library.

Some seed libraries are allowed to sell commercially, and the buyers must agree to NOT save any seeds for years to come.

In Port Townsend, Washington, sits the Organic Seed Alliance, a group of farmers, policy analysts, champions ,and researchers who

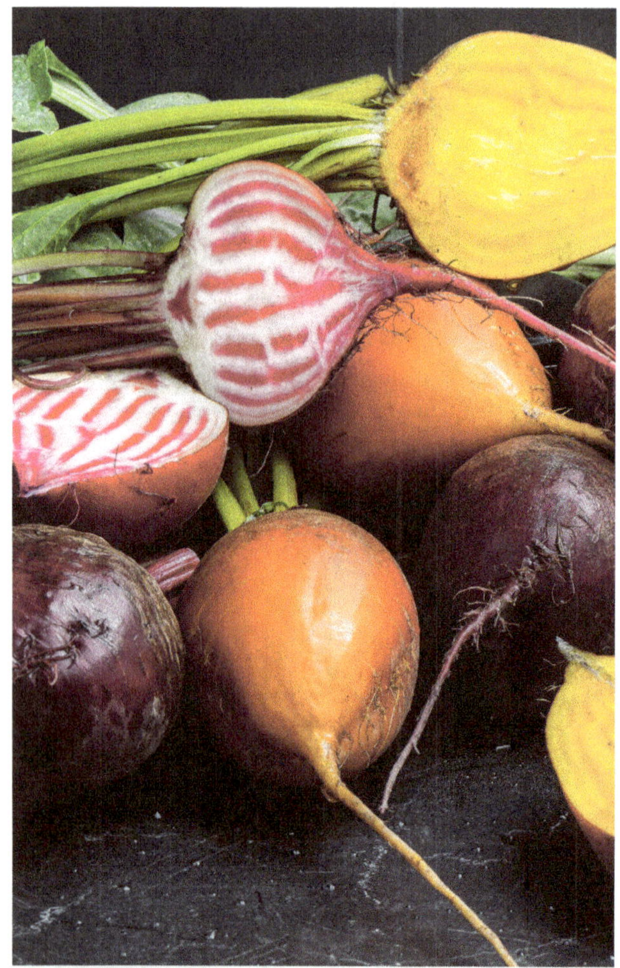

have built a network of partnerships whose mission is to "put the power of seed back into the grower's hands." This 20-year-old organization advocates, researches, learns, and rationalizes [The Federal Seed Act (FSA)](#) and supplemental state law.

Federal law requires seed shipments between States to be labeled with important quality information so seed buyers can make informed choices.

From a high level, the FSA operates amongst cooperative agreements that set the tone for inspection anywhere that seed is sold.

All this data is agreed upon and written into a large Memorandum of Understanding (MOU) to help facilitate and run trueness to variety testing and labeling in seed sales.

The seed records will be tracked for a period of three years with a complete record of the origin, treatment, germination, and purity of each lot of all seeds saved and in production. ∎

HEIRLOOM
PROJECTS

the urban garden project

Based in New Caney, Texas, Charley Fisher is a writer, avid gardener, and founder of [The Urban Garden Project,](#) which led her to do something special for the gardening and farming communities across Texas and the U.S.

Her mission is simple: "to help local residents gain the knowledge they need to secure a food supply for their families."

Hosting gardening workshops, courses, seed saving, and urban farming – Charlie is a dedicated Seed Saver and Food Mover in the Southeast.

Charley's seed catalog is choc full of heirloom beans, tomatoes, peppers, and flowers, with names like [The Kentucky Wonder Bush Bean](#). A bush bean variety matures in just about 55 days. She carries over 300 seed varieties online.■

melon

north yakima

Starting a community garden takes passion and dedication, let alone a program that weaves together environmental farming, science-based teaching to K-12 learners, heirloom saving, and seed library creation.

The Washington State University (WSU) Master Gardener Program in Yakima County did just that! They built a demonstration farm run by students and the WSU community.

This garden program serves over 200 people per month, producing over 2000 pounds of produce each year. WSU Master Gardeners run Six Youth Gardens in low-income neighborhoods, reaching nearly 100 students.

Nearly 830 Yakima County students each year participate in The Youth Environmental Summit, Arborfest and Salvation Army summer camp.

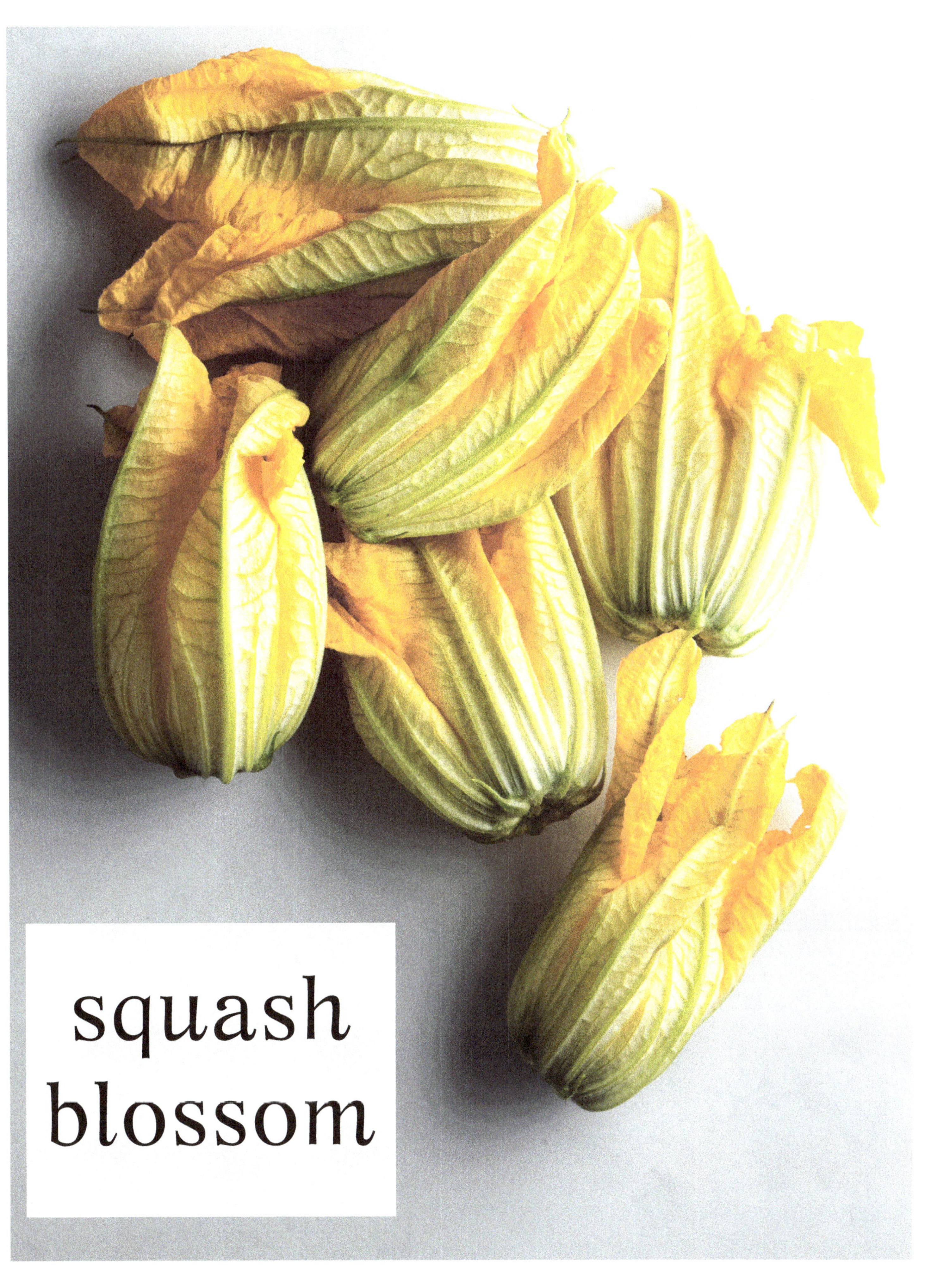

squash
blossom

The program has partnered with the Yakima Nation, where over 100 Native American families participate in community farming and heirloom seed saving.

Locals and the youth have invested more than 1000 hours of work – where over 300 seed packets have been produced and packaged at the Heirloom Garden. Over 1000 seedlings have been produced and distributed to local families to help them grow food.

For information regarding the project, contact Mike Bush, Master Gardener Faculty Lead, WSU Yakima County Extension, 2403 S. 18th. St. Suite 100, Union Gap, WA 98903, call: (509) 574-1600 or email: bushm@wsu.edu.edu. ■

berries

scatterseed project

The [Scatterseed Project](#) focuses on genetic conservation and is located halfway between the Canadian border and Freeport, Maine.

Will Bonsall, a well-known Seed Saver, is dedicated to building biodiversity in our food system. The objective is to connect people with their horticultural heritage. He works to authentically preserve landscapes and the diversity of vegetables, fruits, and flowers.

He authored *Will Bonsall's Essential Guide to Radical Self-Reliant Gardening*, which is his mission to spread seeds of rare and diverse vegetation worldwide.

Will is also one of the directors and original curators of the [Seed Savers Exchange](#) in Decorah, IA. ∎

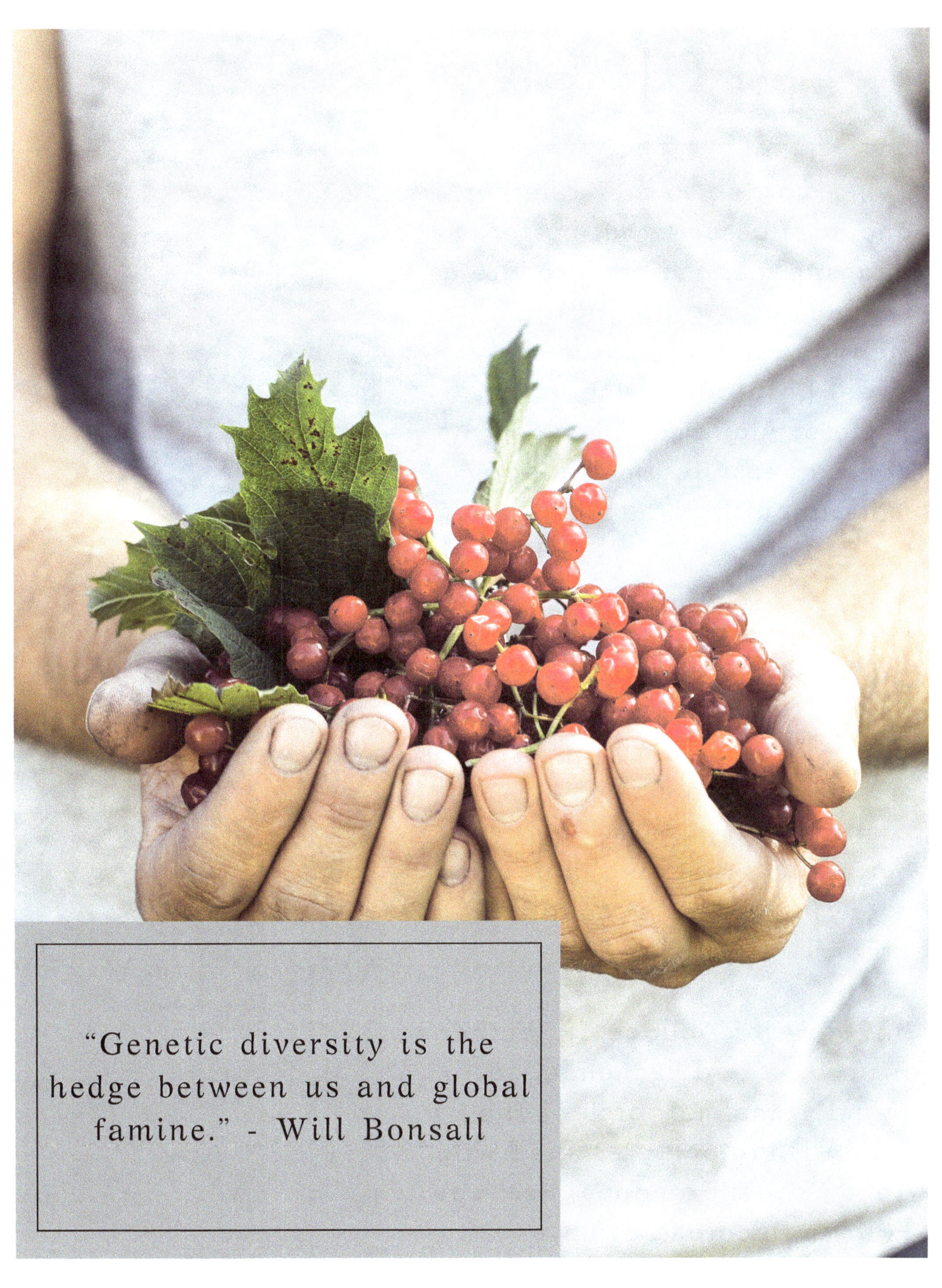

"Genetic diversity is the hedge between us and global famine." - Will Bonsall

the collards project

Being married to a Southerner, one must assume that butter beans, peas, and collards are a big part of our diet, not to mention rainbow chards and sweet potatoes. Living in the State of Alabama—known for its collards—inspired me to learn more about Ira Wallace and The Collards Project.

Growing up on a Connecticut farm, I had experience with collards and the application of Salt Pork. During my research for this book, I heard rumblings that a group of dedicated food movers had recorded and raised over 70 varieties of collard greens.

In 2016 - Ira Wallace of Southern Exposure Seed Exchange, co-founder and matriarch of The Collards Project, partnered with Seed Savers Exchange, Heritage Farm in Decorah, Iowa, to expand the library.

collards

Beginning in North and South Carolina, their mission was to regenerate and share rare heirloom collard seeds with as many people as possible.

A staple in Soul Food, seed savers and food movers are growing these amazing green delights for high-end restaurants with Michelin Stars. This does not exclude the local "Meat and Three," where Southern culture begins with a large side of Collards and a cornbread slab.

This project doesn't stop in the Carolinas. Ira Wallace and her partners have created a groundswell so far and so deep that roots have taken hold from Maine to The State of Washington.

This project is partially responsible for the growth of today's Black American farmers, millennials, and Gen Z's, taking it to the next level.

People are growing greens with names like Old Timey Blue-59 and Morris Header-47. We should also learn about Chef Adam Howard's Braised Field Greens with White Soy Pot Likker, served at his restaurant, Blue Duck Tavern. ■

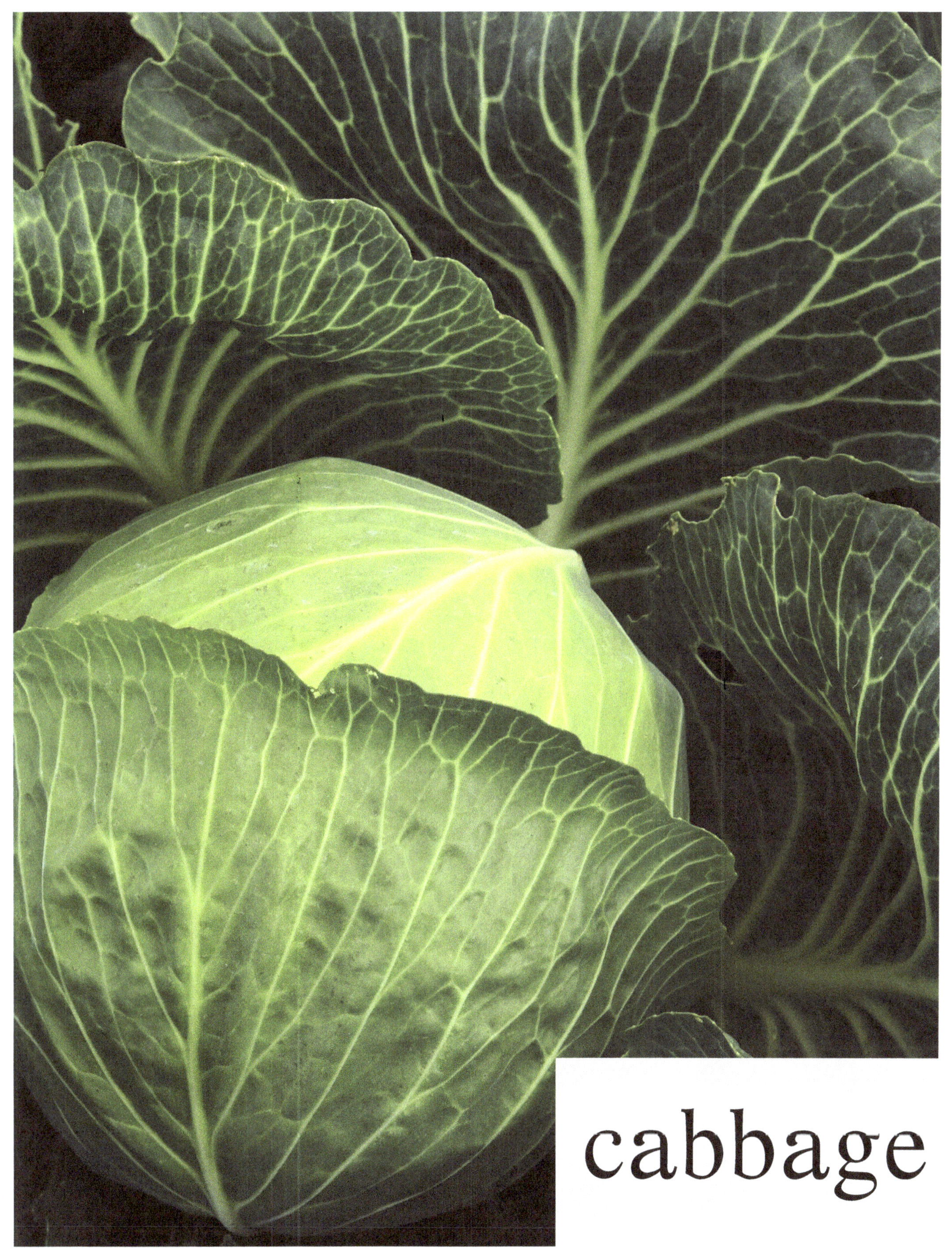

cabbage

heirloom corn

Some say there are over 12,000 heirloom varieties of open-pollinated corn. Heirloom seed-saving projects, which focus on saving our legacies, are gaining momentum around the world.

All of these landraces can be genetically traced back to the domestication of maize in southern Mexico around 9,000 years ago (Van Heerwaardena, et al. 2011).

In 2004, Anthony Martin Belsito wrote his Master's Thesis on Open Pollinated Corn Variety Trials and a Discussion On The Practical Implications For Open Pollinated Corn In Small Scale Whiskey Production.

Putting heirloom corn back into the supply chain in a scalable fashion. Exploring the profit margins of a large corporation, with the benefits of saving seeds important to our culture.

corn

Another important project, called [Masienda](#), has been empowering heirloom corn farmers in Oaxaca, Mexico, since 2014.

Bringing family farmers together in a cooperative of sorts to cultivate heritage and heirloom corn, selling it to chefs and curators worldwide, and making some of the most nutritious and delicious recipes using heirloom maize.

The Dudley Family White Heirloom Corn from Newberry, Florida, was revived by the [Work Food Seed Collective from Gainsville, Florida](#).

Over the years, as the Dudleys planted during the summer rains in June, they cultivated a durable and flavorful breed of white heirloom corn.

In 2019, Rachelle Halaska from the University of Wisconsin-Milwaukee wrote [Heirloom and Hybrid Corn in the American Corn Belt: an Ethnography of Seed-Saving Practices](#) which examines the practices and context of contemporary heirloom corn seed-saving practices and projects in the American Corn Belt.

Her thesis examined heirloom corn conservation and hand-pollination practices at the Seed Savers Exchange in Decorah, Iowa 2015, studying bagging, bulking, and hand-pollinating heirloom corn varieties.

As we move into deeper levels of the organic food movement, the practice of saving seeds feeds us and reminds us of the farmers and growers before us who worked hard at preserving history. ■

the okra project

To some, okra is not a daily staple in their diets. However, it is a vegetable that is becoming more common in dishes at your favorite corner diner and even some Michelin Star restaurants like London's, Tamarind run by Peter Joseph, who is buying heirloom okra to make some amazing dishes. Aloo Bhindi Bhujiya is a dish made with okra and potatoes, maximizing flavor and food anthropology.

Growers and land stewards all are spending time learning more about the history of okra, its cultural heritage, and growing heirloom okra on farms to improve its resilience, broaden offerings, and overall awareness.

Organizations like The Utopian Seed Project are creating awareness of heirlooms and seed diversity, saving dozens of varieties – building a platform of diverse and genetically resilient plants.

okra

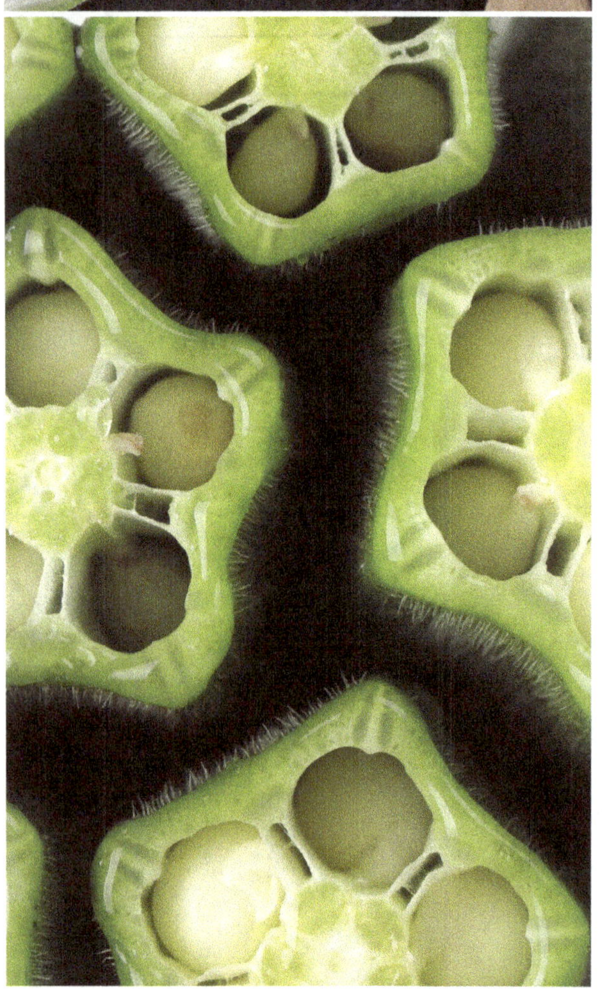

Okra is native to Africa and a staple of the deep south. Chris Smith, the executive director of [The Utopian Seed Project](#) and author of [The Whole Okra](#) - is passionate about creating a meaningful approach to okra and its flavor profiles. The Okra project inspired him to become obsessed with breaking the stigma around [okra](#) and its versatility and nutritional values.

Over 250 farms across the United States are working to promote crop diversity and sustainable food production. Notable projects are the [Whidby White Community Seed Selection Project](#), the [Utopian Seed Project](#), and [The Native Seeds/SEARCH](#) in Tuscon, Arizona.

Some examples of varieties to look for are Red Burgundy, which produces red pods etched with green tips. Clemson University developed this variety. Another is The Hill Country Heirloom Red - bright red hues with an earthen flavor profile. Finally, The Cow Horn is crunchy and good for pickling.

For more information about okra, contact The Utopian Seed Project. ∎

SEED COMPANIES

Heirloom & Heritage Seeds

Family Owned

notable heirloom companies

[Eden Brothers Seed Company](#) of Arden, North Carolina, carries 62 heirloom tomato seed varieties. From the Roma VF, a likely tomato for pastes and sauces, to Green Zebra, incredible for a slicer on sammies or salads. If ordering high volume, above a few seed packets, they sell some tomato seeds by the ounce.

[The True Leaf Market](#) sells 232 heirloom and open-pollinated tomato seeds. When shopping online, the varieties can be overwhelming – so shop with intention and pick recipes to accompany your buying decisions. Or, plant several varieties to see which ones grow the best in your garden. When researching, their staff has done a great job writing descriptions with downloadable growing guides for your digital library.

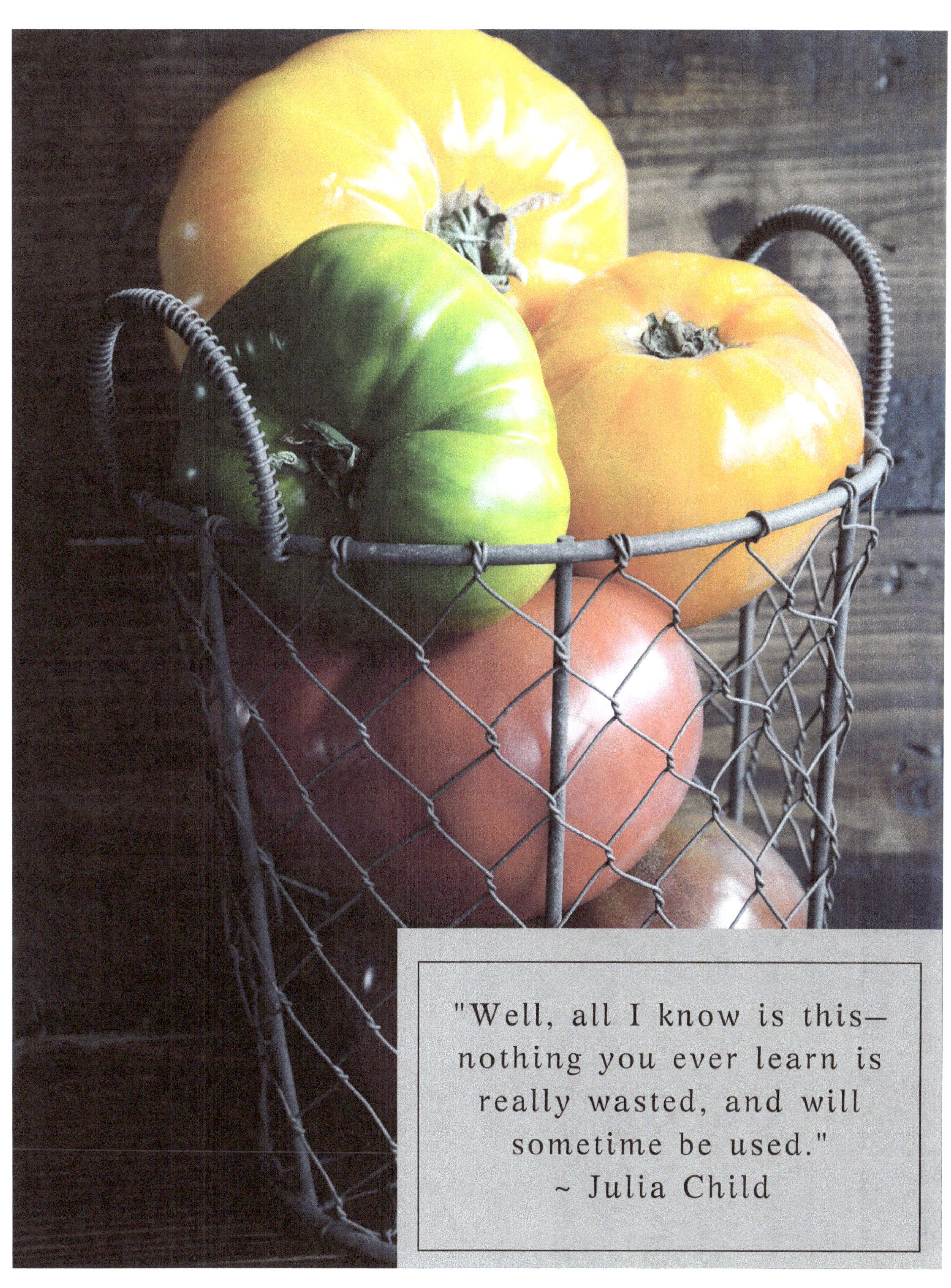
"Well, all I know is this—
nothing you ever learn is
really wasted, and will
sometime be used."
~ Julia Child

The [Seed Nerds Company](#) offers 41 varieties of heirloom tomatoes, and one of the more exciting seeds is their [Tomatillo Purple Tomato Heirloom Seeds](#). An open-pollinated and Non-GMO seed - this flavorful fruit offers a tasty alternative to the traditional varieties when considering homemade salsa. Roast them in cast iron and seal them off when hot to capture the earthen flavors.

[Thresh Seed Company](#) -based in Guthrie County, Iowa - Becky and Dave Weeks founded Thresh Seed Company, carrying on a 140-year legacy of their family farming operation. They carry over 60 varieties of heirloom seeds available for sale. The [Mortgage Lifter](#) is a unique heirloom variety from West Virginia that ultimately paid off the breeder's mortgage. Their descriptions are super and contain a detailed "Grows Well With" section.

Contact [Becky](#) with any questions you might have regarding seeds or purchasing by volume.

Annie's Heirlooms Seeds not only shares its offerings, but it also shares product reviews, offering a real-world perspective on propagating, growing, and harvesting.

For example, The Rainbow Cherry Collection offers five types of heirloom cherry tomato seeds. This particular collection includes a collection of 10 seeds each: Chadwick Cherry Tomato (red) Chocolate Cherry Tomato (black) Golden Nugget Cherry Tomato (gold) Snow White Cherry Tomato (pale yellow) Yellow Pear Tomato (yellow). Contact customer service if you have any questions about their seeds or products.

Parker Ford, Pennsylvania, is home to Bucktown Seed Company, selling open-pollinated non-GMO seeds with wonderful naming conventions and beautiful backstories: Jeff, a photographer with a passion for farming, and wife Christa, an educator and health advocate. 2024 brings their customers 23 heirloom tomato seed offerings—a flair for a beautifully detailed description, accompanied by growing tips and seed facts.

They carefully curate and photograph their stock. Most seed packets come with 25 seeds, so don't forget to check out the Supplies section. Contact customer service to ask questions regarding volume purchases or tracking down some interesting breeds.

The Hudson Valley Seed Company has a fantastic array of seed offerings, equipment, and downloadable catalogs for those who want the analog version. I enjoy printing and/or ordering a seed catalog, making notes and lists when planning to grow beds for flowers, and environmental landscaping. They have some eye-catching artwork on their Social media and throughout their website. They are also selling Shumei Natural Agriculture seed collections, a holistic Japanese method of environmental farming. As for heirloom tomatoes, in 2024, offering 57 varieties of tomatoes. Cesare's Canestrino Di Lucca Tomato, an Italian sauce tomato, cooks up delicious earthen and fruity flavor with a bit of dryness. Contact their Home & Garden customer service department for any questions you might have.■

DIRECTORY

ADAPTIVE SEEDS

☎ (541) 367-1105

✉ seed@adaptiveseeds.com

📍 Sweet Home, Oregon

🌐 https://adaptiveseeds.com

AMERICAN MEADOWS

☎ (802) 227-7200

✉ helpdesk@americanmeadows.com

📍 2438 Shelburne Rd. Shelburne, Vermont

🌐 https://americanmeadows.com

AMISHLAND HEIRLOOM SEEDS

☎ (541) 367-1105

✉ lisa@amishlandseeds.com

📍 Reamstown, Pennsylvania

🌐 https://www.facebook.com/amishlandseeds

ANNIE'S HEIRLOOM SEEDS

☎ (888)-575-7853

✉ cs@anniesheirloomseeds.com

◉ 5617 Odana Road Madison, WI

🌐 https://www.anniesheirloomseeds.com

APPALACHIAN HEIRLOOM PLANT FARM

☎ (541) 367-1105

✉ alwest_83@yahoo.com

◉ 16364 State Route 136, Winchester, OH,

🌐 https://www.facebook.com/appalachian heirloomplantfarm

APPLEWOOD SEED COMPANY

☎ (303) 431-7333

✉ sales@applewoodseed.com

◉ 5380 Vivian Street Arvada, CO

🌐 https://adaptiveseeds.com

BAKER CREEK
HEIRLOOM SEEDS

☎ (541) 367-1105

✉ seeds@rareseeds.com

◎ 2278 Baker Creek Road, Mansfield, MO

🌐 https://www.rareseeds.com

BBB SEED
COMPANY

☎ (303) 530-1222

✉ info@BBBseed.com

◎ 6595 Odell Pl STE G, Boulder, CO

🌐 https://bbbseed.com

BEAR CREEK
FARM

☎ (855) 466-2836

✉ hana@bearcreekfarm.com

◎ 108 Hunns Lake Rd, Bangall, NY

🌐 https://bearcreekfarm.com

BOTANICAL INTERESTS

☎ (877)-821-4340

✉ customerservice@botanicalinterests.com

◎ 660 Compton St., Broomfield, CO

🌐 https://www.botanicalinterests.com/

BUCKTOWN SEED COMPANY

☎ (303) 530-1222

✉ support@bucktownseed.com

◎ 1355 Old Schuylkill Rd Parker Ford, PA

🌐 https://bucktownseed.com

BROWN ENVELOPE SEEDS

☎ (083)-187-4637

✉ madsmckeever@gmail.com

◎ Ardagh, Church Cross, Co. Cork, Ireland

🌐 https://brownenvelopeseeds.ie

CHILE PLANTS

☎ (303) 530-1222

✉ info@chileplants.com

⊙ Hunterdon County, New Jersey

🌐 https://www.chileplants.com/

CLEAR CREEK SEEDS

☎ (918)-871-2701

✉ customerservice@clearcreekseeds.com

⊙ *P.O. Box 703 Hulbert, OK*

🌐 https://www.clearcreekseeds.com

COMMONWEALTH SEEDS

☎ (303) 530-1222

✉ info@chileplants.com

⊙ Hunterdon County, New Jersey

🌐 https://www.chileplants.com/

CRISPY FARMS

 crispyfarms@gmail.com
 Apopka, FL, United States, Florida
 https://www.crispyfarms.com

CUCUMBER SHOP

 info@cucumbershop.com

 *371 Marigold Dr. Fairfield, CA*

 https://cucumbershop.com/

CULTIVARIABLE

 help24@cultivariable.com

 PO Box 111 Moclips, WA 98562

 https://www.cultivariable.com/

D. LANDRETH SEED COMPANY

 (877)-385-4989

 help@landrethseed.com

 Shelburne, VT

 https://www.landrethseed.com

DAGGAWALLA SEEDS AND HERBS

 (805)-758-3184

 daggawalla@riseup.net

 Gila River Valley, New Mexico

 https://daggawalla.com

DAVID'S GARDEN SEEDS

 (210) 502-3797

 davidsgardenseeds@outlook.com

 5029 FM 2504 Poteet, TX

 https://davidsgardenseeds.com/

DEEP HARVEST FARM

 503 989-8490

 seeds@deepharvestfarm.com

 PO Box 515 Freeland, WA

 https://deepharvestfarm.com

DIANE'S FLOWER SEEDS

 dianelinsley@protonmail.com

 https://www.dianeseeds.com

DAVID'S GARDEN SEEDS

☎ (210) 502-3797

✉ davidsgardenseeds@outlook.com

⦿ 5029 FM 2504 Poteet, TX

🌐 https://davidsgardenseeds.com/

DEEP HARVEST FARM

☎ (503)-989-8490

✉ seeds@deepharvestfarm.com

⦿ PO Box 515 Freeland, WA

🌐 https://deepharvestfarm.com

DIANE'S FLOWER SEEDS

☎

✉  dianelinsley@protonmail.com

⦿ 

🌐 https://www.dianeseeds.com

DIRT GOODNESS SUPER SEEDS

5029 FM 2504 Poteet, TX

https://www.dirtgoddessseeds.com

ED HUME SEEDS

(253)-435-4897

info@humeseeds.com

11504 58th Ave E, Puyallup, WA

https://humeseeds.com/

EDEN BROTHERS

(855)-440-2929

service@edenbrothers.com

2099 Brevard Rd., Arden, NC

https://www.edenbrothers.com/

EDIBLE VENTURA COUNTY

☎ (805) 705-9550

✉ orders@plantgoodseed.com

📍 226 West Ojai Ave Ste 101-539 Ojai, CA

🌐 https://edibleventuracounty.ediblecommunities.com/guide/all-good-things-organic-seeds

EXPERIMENTAL FARM NETWORK

☎ (253)-435-4897

✉ nathankleinman@gmail.com

📍 Philadelphia, PA

🌐 https://www.experimentalfarmnetwork.org

FARM DIRECT SEED

☎ (719)-250-9835

✉ info@puebloseed.com

📍 25 N. Beech St. Cortez, CO

🌐 https://farmdirectseed.com

FEDCO SEEDS

☎ (207)-426-9900

✉ questions@fedcoseeds.com

📍 PO Box 520 Clinton, ME

🌐 https://www.fedcoseeds.com/

FERRY MORSE

☎ (508)-928-4769

✉ info@ferrymorse.com

📍 202 S Washington St., Norton MA

🌐 https://ferrymorse.com/

FILAREE GARLIC FARM

☎ (509)-422-6940

✉ info@filareefarm.com

📍 25 N. Beech St. Cortez, CO

🌐 https://filareefarm.com/

FLORET FLOWER FARM

support@floretflowers.com

P.O. Box 281 Mount Vernon, WA

https://www.floretflowers.com/

FOUNDROOT

(907)-314-2014

info@foundroot.com

PO BOX 1174 HAINES, AK 99827

https://foundroot.com

FRUITION SEEDS

(585)-374-8903

support@fruitionseeds.com

7921 Hickory Bottom Road Naples, NY

https://fruitionseeds.com/

GARDNER BASICS

☎ (801)-769-6181

✉ info@gardenersbasics.com

📍 3573 North Main Street Spanish Fork, U

🌐 https://www.gardenersbasics.com/

GILBERT H. WILD & SON

☎ (888)-449-4537

✉ customerservice@gilberthwild.com

📍 2944 State Highway 37, Reeds, MO

🌐 https://gilberthwild.com/

GOOD SEED COMPANY

☎ (406)-471-3284

✉ seeds@goodseedco.net

📍 Riverside Plaza, 100 Second Street East, Ste 305, Whitefish, MT,

🌐 goodseedco

GOT TINY SEEDS

☏ (508)-231-6417

✉ customerservice@gottinyseeds.com

⚲ P.O. Box 265 Millis, MA

🌐 https://www.gottinyseeds.com/

GOURMET SEED

☏ (831)-637.2411

✉ customerservice@gourmetseed.com

⚲ 743 Shore Road, CA, 95023-9427

🌐 https://www.gourmetseed.com/

GREEN HAVEN

☏ (607)-566-9253

✉ opcorn@gmail.com

⚲ 8225 Wessels Hill Road Avoca, NY

🌐 https://openpollinated.com

GROW ORGANIC

 (888)-784-1722

 helpdesk@groworganic.com

 125 Clydesdale Ct. Grass Valley, CA

 https://www.groworganic.com

GROWER JIM'S
PLANTS & PRODUCE

 (831)-637-2411

 growerjim@facebook.com

 Orlando, FL

 growerjim.blogspot.com

GURNEYS

 (513)-354-1492

 service@gurneys.com

 P.O. Box 4178 Lawrenceburg, IN

 https://www.gurneys.com/

HARRIS SEEDS

☎ (888)-784-1722

✉ salestaxexempt@harrisseeds.com

⚲ 355 Paul Rd Rochester, NY

🌐 https://www.harrisseeds.com

HARVESTING HISTORY

☎ (410)-627-6831

✉ bmelera@harvesting-history.com

⚲ 109 Lexie Lane, Kill Devil Hills, NC

🌐 https://harvesting-history.com

HAWAII SEED GROWERS NETWORK

☎ (513)-354-1492

✉ hawaiiseedgrowersnetwork@gmail.com

⚲

🌐 https://www.hawaiiseedgrowersnetwork.com

HIGH COUNTRY GARDENS

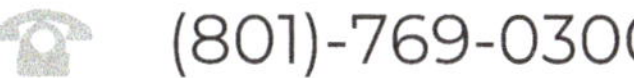

☎ (801)-769-0300

✉ plants@highcountrygardens.com

📍 6921 Pan American Fwy NE, Albuquerque

🌐 https://www.highcountrygardens.com

HIGH MOWING ORGANIC SEEDS

☎ (802)-472-6174

✉ questions@highmowingseeds.com

📍 76 Quarry Road Wolcott, VT

🌐 https://www.highmowingseeds.com

HOMETOWN SEEDS

☎ (435)-881-5861

✉ info@hometownseeds.com

📍 507 N. 1500 W. Orem, Utah

🌐 https://www.hometownseeds.com/

HOME-GROWN SEEDS

 (718)-682-2607

 help@homegrown-garden.com

120 East Main Street, Box #127, Ramsey NJ

 https://homegrown-garden.com/

HUDSON VALLEY SEED LIBRARY

 (845)-204-8769

 mail@hudsonvalleyseed.com

4737 US 209, Accord, NY,

 https://www.hudsonvalleyseeds.com

IRISH EYES GARDEN SEEDS

 (509)-933-7150 Option 2

 customerservice@irisheyesgardenseeds.com

5045 Robinson Canyon Road, Ellensburg WA

 https://irisheyesgardenseeds.com

ITALIAN GARDEN SEEDS

☎ (705) 718-3499

✉ danielb@italiangardenseeds.com

◉ Alliston, Ontario, Canada

🌐 https://www.italiangardenseeds.com

JOHNNY'S SELECTED SEEDS

☎ (877)-564-6697

✉ service@johnnyseeds.com

◉ 955 Benton Ave Winslow, ME

🌐 https://www.johnnyseeds.com

JUNG SEED COMPANY

☎ (800)-297-3123

✉ info@jungseed.com

◉ 335 S. High St. Randolph, WI

🌐 https://www.jungseed.com

KITCHEN GARDEN SEEDS

☎ (860)-567-6086

✉ customerservice@kitchengardenseds.com

⚲ 23 Tulip Drive P.O. Box 638 Bantam, CT

🌐 https://www.kitchengardenseds.com

LANDRETH SEED

☎ (877)-385-4989

✉ help@landrethseed.com

⚲ Pennsylvania

🌐 https://www.landrethseed.com

LONGFIELD GARDENS

☎ (855)-534-2733

✉ info@lfgardens.com

⚲ 1245 Airport Rd Lakewood, NJ

🌐 https://www.longfield-gardens.com

MASIENDA

☎ (213)-435-9037

✉ 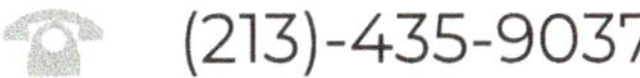info@masienda.com

◉ 11515 West Pico Blvd., Los Angeles, CA

🌐 https://masienda.com

MARY'S HEIRLOOM SEEDS

☎ (903)-833-7333

✉ 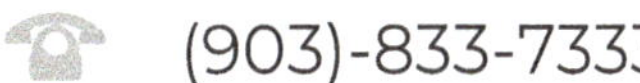mary@marysheirloomseeds.com

◉ P.O. Box 593 Ben Wheeler, TX

🌐 https://www.marysheirloomseeds.com

MEADOW LARK HEARTH

☎ (308)-631-5877

✉ meadowlarkhearth@gmail.com

◉ 120024 Everett Dr, Scottsbluff, NE

🌐 https://www.longfield-gardens.com

MI GARDENER

 (810)-300-8845

 contact@migardener.com

 1426 Oakland St St Clair, MI

 https://migardener.com

MONTICELLO SHOP

 (800)-243-0743

 catalog@monticello.org

 931 Thomas Jefferson Pwy, Charlottesville

 https://monticelloshop.org

MOUNTAIN ROSE HERBS

 (308)-631-5877

 support@mountainroseherbs.com

 4060 Stewart Rd, Eugene, OR

 https://mountainroseherbs.com

NATIVE SEEDS

 (520)-622-0830

 orders@nativeseeds.org

 3584 E River Rd Tucson, AZ

 https://www.nativeseeds.org

NATURE AND NURTURE SEEDS

 (734)-929-0802

 info@natureandnurtureseeds.com

 7100 Marshall Rd. Dexter, MI

 https://natureandnurtureseeds.com

NESEED

 (800)-825-5477

 sales@neseed.com

 122 Park Ave., Building H, East Hartford, CT

 https://www.neseed.com

NORTH CIRCLE SEEDS

 (631)-807-5163

 zachary@northcircleseeds.com

 26253 485th Street Vergas, MN

 https://northcircleseeds.com

NOURSE FARMS

 (413)-665-2658

 info@noursefarms.com

 41 River Road Whately, MA

 https://noursefarms.com

OHIO HEIRLOOM SEEDS

 (614)-554-4657

 michael@dehlendorf.com

 1024 Amberly Place Columbus, OH

 https://ohioheirloomseeds.com

OPEN CIRCLE SEEDS

 (707)-354-3991

 info@opencircleseeds.com

 PO Box 81 Potter Valley, CA

 https://www.opencircleseeds.com

OSBORN QUALITY SEED

 (413)-665-2658

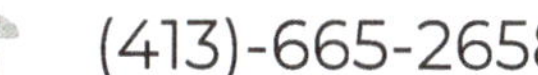 info@osborneseed.com

 PO Box 1647 Mount Vernon, WA

 https://www.osborneseed.com

OUTSIDE PRIDE

 (800)-670-4192

 support@outsidepride.com

 Willamette Valley, OR

 https://www.outsidepride.com

PARK SEED

 (800)-845-3369

 parkwholesale@parkseed.com

 One Parkton Avenue Greenwood, SC

 https://parkseed.com

PEACEFUL HERITIAGE NURSERY

 (859)-319-9228

 order@peacefulheritage.com

 Kentucky

 https://peacefulheritage.com/

PEPPER JOE'S

 (888)-660-2276

 customerservice@pepperjoe.com

 Myrtle Beach, South Carolina

 https://pepperjoe.com/

PINETREE GARDEN SEEDS & ACCESSORIES

 (207)-926-3400

 help@superseeds.com

 PO Box 300 New Gloucester, ME

 https://www.superseeds.com

PRAIRIE MOON NURSERY

 (866)-417-8156

 info@prairiemoon.com

 32115 Prairie Lane Winona, MN

 https://www.prairiemoon.com

PRAIRIE ROAD ORGANIC

 (701)-883-4416

 info@prairieroadorganic.co

 Fullerton, ND

 https://www.prairieroadorganic.co/

QUAIL SEEDS

 quailseeds@gmail.com

 Eel River, CA

 https://www.quailseeds.com/

R.H. SHUMWAY'S

 (800)-342-9461

 info@rhshumway.com

 334 W. Stroud St. Randolph, WI

 https://www.rhshumway.com/

RARE SEEDS

 (701)-883-4416

 seeds@rareseeds.com

 2278 Baker Creek Road, Mansfield, MO

 https://www.rareseeds.com/

REDWOOD SEEDS

☎ (530)-524-5537

✉ 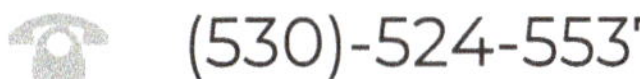 info@redwoodseeds.net

◎ PO Box 431 Manton, CA

🌐 https://www.redwoodseeds.net/

REIMER SEEDS

☎ (800)-342-9461

✉ 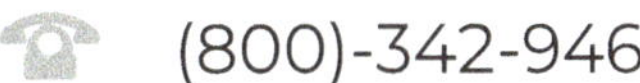 mail@reimerseeds.com

◎  PO Box 206, Saint Leonard, MD

🌐  https://www.reimerseeds.com/

RENEES GARDEN

☎ (888)-880-7228

✉ renee@reneesgarden.com

◎ 6060 Graham Hill Rd. Felton, CA

🌐 https://www.reneesgarden.com/

RESILIENT SEEDS

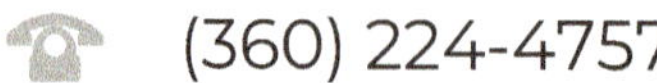

☎ (360) 224-4757

✉ backyardbeans@gmail.com

📍 2356 E Hemmi RD Bellingham, WA

🌐 https://www.resilientseeds.com/

RESTORATION SEEDS

☎ (541)-535-3532

✉ orders@restorationseeds.com

📍 9969 Wagner Creek Road Talent, OR

🌐 https://www.restorationseeds.com/

ROHRER SEEDS

☎ (717)-299-2571

✉ info@rohrerseeds.com

📍 2472 Old Philadelphia Pike, Lancaster, PA

🌐 https://rohrerseeds.com/

ROUNDSTONE NATIVE SEEDS

 (888)-531-2353

 sales@roundstoneseed.com

 9764 Raider Hollow Road Upton, Ky

 https://roundstoneseed.com/

ROW 7 SEED CO.

 (914)-510-2824

 info@row7seeds.com

 PO Box 89, Dobbs Ferry, New York, NY

 https://www.row7seeds.com/

SAN DIEGO SEED COMPANY

 (858)-203-1273

 info@sandiegoseedcompany.com

 San Diego, CA

 https://sandiegoseedcompany.com

SCATTERED PROJECT SEED BANK

☎ (800)-626-0866

✉ WABonsall@gmail.com

◎ 39 Bailey Road, Industry, ME

🌐 https://www.scatterseedproject.org/

SECRET SEED CARTEL

☎ (914)-510-2824

✉ Terry@Secretseedcartel.com

◎ Magland, France

🌐 https://secretseedcartel.com/

SEEDS FOR GENERATIONS

☎ (855)-625-4769

✉ generation@gmail.com

◎ PO Box 60, Newport, Virginia

🌐 http://seedsforgenerations.com/

SEED MAIL

Contact@seedmailseed.co

https://www.seedmailseed.co/

SEED NERDS

(716)-217-9642

info@seednerds.com

11010 Juniper Ave, Fontana, CA

https://seednerds.com/

SEED REVOLUTION NOW

(855)-625-4769

moriainsantafe@yahoo.com

San Mateo, California,

https://seedrevolutionnow.blogspot.com

SEED SAVERS EXCHANGE

 (563)-382-5990

 customerservice@seedsavers.org

 3094 North Winn Road Decorah, IA

 https://seedsavers.org

SEED SNOW

 (716)-217-9642

 info@seedsnow.com

 West Hollywood, CA

 https://www.seedsnow.com

SEED TREASURES

 moriainsantafe@yahoo.com

 8533 Hwy 25, Angora, MN

 https://seedtreasures.com

SEEDS FROM ITALY

 (785)-748-0959

 seeds@growitalian.com

 PO Box 3908 Lawrence, KS

 https://www.growitalian.com

SEEDS OF THE PRAIRIE

 (804)-716-2089

 johndoleman@soc-cr.org

 West Hollywood, CA

 https://www.seedsofchange.com

SEEDS-N-SUCH

 (706)-305-9751

 service@seedsnsuch.com

 P.O. Box 1777, Augusta, GA

 https://seedsnsuch.com/

SELECT SEEDS

 (800)-684-0395

 customerservice@selectseeds.com

 180 Stickney Hill Road, Union, CT

 https://www.selectseeds.com

SISKIYOU SEEDS

 (541)-415-0877

 info@siskiyouseeds.com

 3220 East Fork Rd., Williams, OR

 https://www.siskiyouseeds.com/

SNAKE RIVER SEED COOPERATIVE

(208)-996-3531

info@snakeriverseeds.com

Boise, ID

https://snakeriverseeds.com

SOUTH GEORGIA SEED COMPANY

✉ customerservice@southgaseedco.com

📍 Blue Ridge Mountains of North GA

🌐 https://stores.southgaseedco.com/

SOUTHERN EXPOSURE SEED EXCHANGE

 (540)-894-9480

 gardens@southernexposure.com

 P.O. Box 460 Mineral, Virginia

 https://www.siskiyouseeds.com/

SOW TRUE SEED

 (208)-996-3531

 info@sowtrue.com

 243 Haywood St., Asheville, NC

 https://sowtrueseed.com

ST. CLARE SEEDS

 email@stclareseeds.com
 P.O. Box 254 Bedford, MI
 https://www.stclareseeds.com

STOVER SEED

 (213)-626-9668
 customer_service@stoverseed.com
 California
 https://www.stoverseed.com/

STRICTLY MEDICINAL SEEDS

 (541)-846-0872
 ordersupport@strictlymedicinalseeds.com
 PO Box 299 Williams, OR
 https://strictlymedicinalseeds.com

SUNDIAL SEED

Willits, CA

https://permies.com/wiki/76739/Sundial-Seed-Company-California-USA

SUNFLOWER STEVE

info@sunflowersteve.com

Wisconsin

https://sunflowersteveseedco.com

SUPER SEEDS (PINETREE GARDEN SEEDS)

(207)-926-3400

hello@superseeds.com

PO Box 300 New Gloucester, ME

https://www.superseeds.com/

SUSTAINABLE MOUNTAIN AGRICULTURE

 (252)-368-6556

 smac@heirlooms.org

 131 Main Street Gatesville, NC

 https://www.heirlooms.org

TERRIOR SEEDS

 (888)-878-5247

 Seeds@UnderwoodGardens.com

 P O Box 4995 Chino Valley, AZ

 https://underwoodgardens.com

TERRITORIAL SEED COMPANY

 (800)-626-0866

 info@territorialseed.com

 PO Box 158 | Cottage Grove, OR

 https://territorialseed.com

THE GARDENER'S WORKSHOP

 (757)-877-7159

 info@thegardenersworkshop.com

 Newport News, VA

 www.www.thegardenersworkshop.com

THE MAINE POTATO LADY

 (888)-878-5247

 customerservice@mainepotatolady.com

 PO Box 65 Guilford, ME

 https://www.mainepotatolady.com

THE NAKED SEED COMPANY

 (817)-557-2121

 info@nakedseedcompany.com

 Newport, New Hampshire

 https://nakedseedcompany.com

THE GARDENER'S WORKSHOP

 (757)-877-7159

 info@thegardenersworkshop.com

 Newport News, VA

 www.www.thegardenersworkshop.com

THE MAINE POTATO LADY

 (888)-878-5247

 customerservice@mainepotatolady.com

 PO Box 65 Guilford, ME

 https://www.mainepotatolady.com

THE NAKED SEED COMPANY

 (817)-557-2121

 info@nakedseedcompany.com

 Newport, New Hampshire

 https://nakedseedcompany.com

THE SEED GUY

 (918)-352-8800

 linda@theseedguy.com

 Bella Vista, AR

 https://theseedguy.net

THE TASTEFUL GARDEN

 (678)-818-9154

 mail@tastefulgarden.com

 County Road 561 Woodland, AL

 https://tastefulgarden.com

THE UTOPIAN SEED PROJECT

 admin@theutopianseedproject.org

 Asheville, NC

 https://theutopianseedproject.org

TODD'S SEEDS

 (248)-206-3200

 info@toddsseeds.com

 Livonia, MI

 https://toddsseeds.com

TOMATO FEST

 (641)-524-5832

 gary@tomatofest.com

 https://www.tomatofest.com

TOMATO GROWERS SUPPLY COMPANY

 (239)-768-1119

 customerservice@tomatogrowers.com

 Fort Myers, FL

 https://tomatogrowers.com

TOTALLY TOMATOES

 (800)-345-5977

 info@totallytomato.com

 Randolph, WI

 https://www.totallytomato.com

TRADE WINDS FRUIT

 service@tradewindsfruit.com

 PO Box 9396 Santa Rosa, CA

 https://www.totallytomato.com

TRUE LEAF MARKET

 (801)-491-8700

 support@trueleafmarket.com

 Salt Lake City, Utah

 https://www.trueleafmarket.com

TURTLE TREE BIODYNAMIC SEED INITIATIVE

orders@trueloveseeds.com

PO Box 12648 Philadelphia, PA

https://trueloveseeds.com

TWO SEEDS IN A POD

contact@twoseedsinapod.com

Masontown, WV

https://twoseedsinapod.com

UJAMAA SEEDS

ujamaafarmingcoop@gmail.com

https://ujamaaseeds.com

UPRISING ORGANICS

 (360)-778-3749

 info@uprisingorganics.com

 BELLINGHAM, WA

 https://uprisingorganics.com

URBAN GARDEN PROJECT

 (713)-929-6462

 contact@urbangardenproject.com

 Houston, Texas

 https://www.urbangardenproject.com

URBAN FARMER

 (317)-600-2807

 info@ufseeds.com

 Westfield, IN

 https://www.ufseeds.com

VERMONT BEAN SEED CO.

 (800)-349-1071

 info@vermontbean.com

 Randolph, WI

 https://www.vermontbean.com

VESEYS SEEDS

 (800)-363-7333

 customerservice@veseys.com

 Irving, TX

 https://www.veseys.com

VICTORY SEED COMPANY

 (317)-600-2807

 info@ufseeds.com

 Westfield, IN

 https://www.ufseeds.com

VERMONT BEAN SEED CO.

 (800)-349-1071

 info@vermontbean.com

 Randolph, WI

 https://www.vermontbean.com

VESEYS SEEDS

 (800)-363-7333

 customerservice@veseys.com

 411 Hwy 25, York Road, York, Canada

 https://www.veseys.com

VICTORY SEED COMPANY

 (817)-382-8489

 info@victoryseeds.com

 Irving, Texas

 https://www.victoryseeds.com

WEST COAST SEEDS

 (888)-804-8820

 customerservice@westcoastseeds.com

 Vancouver, British Columbia

 https://www.westcoastseeds.com

WHITE EARTH LAND RECOVERY PROJECT

 (218)-375-4602

 WhiteEarthNativeHarvest@gmail.com

 Callaway, MN

 https://www.welrp.org

WILD BOAR FARMS

 (888)-784-1722

 wildboarfarms@hotmail.com

 Citrus Heights, CA

 https://www.wildboarfarms.com

WILD GARDEN SEED

 (541)-929-4068

 karen@wildgardenseed.com

 Philomath, OR

 https://www.wildgardenseed.com

WILD SEED PROJECT

 info@wildseedproject.net

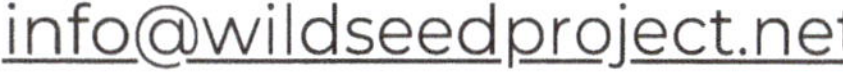

 https://shop.wildseedproject.net

WOOD PRAIRIE FARM

 (207)-429-9765

 orders@woodprairie.com

 Bridgewater, ME

 https://www.woodprairie.com

YONDER HILL FARM

 yonderhillfarm.ca@gmail.com

Lunenburg County, Nova Scotia

https://yonderhillfarm.ca

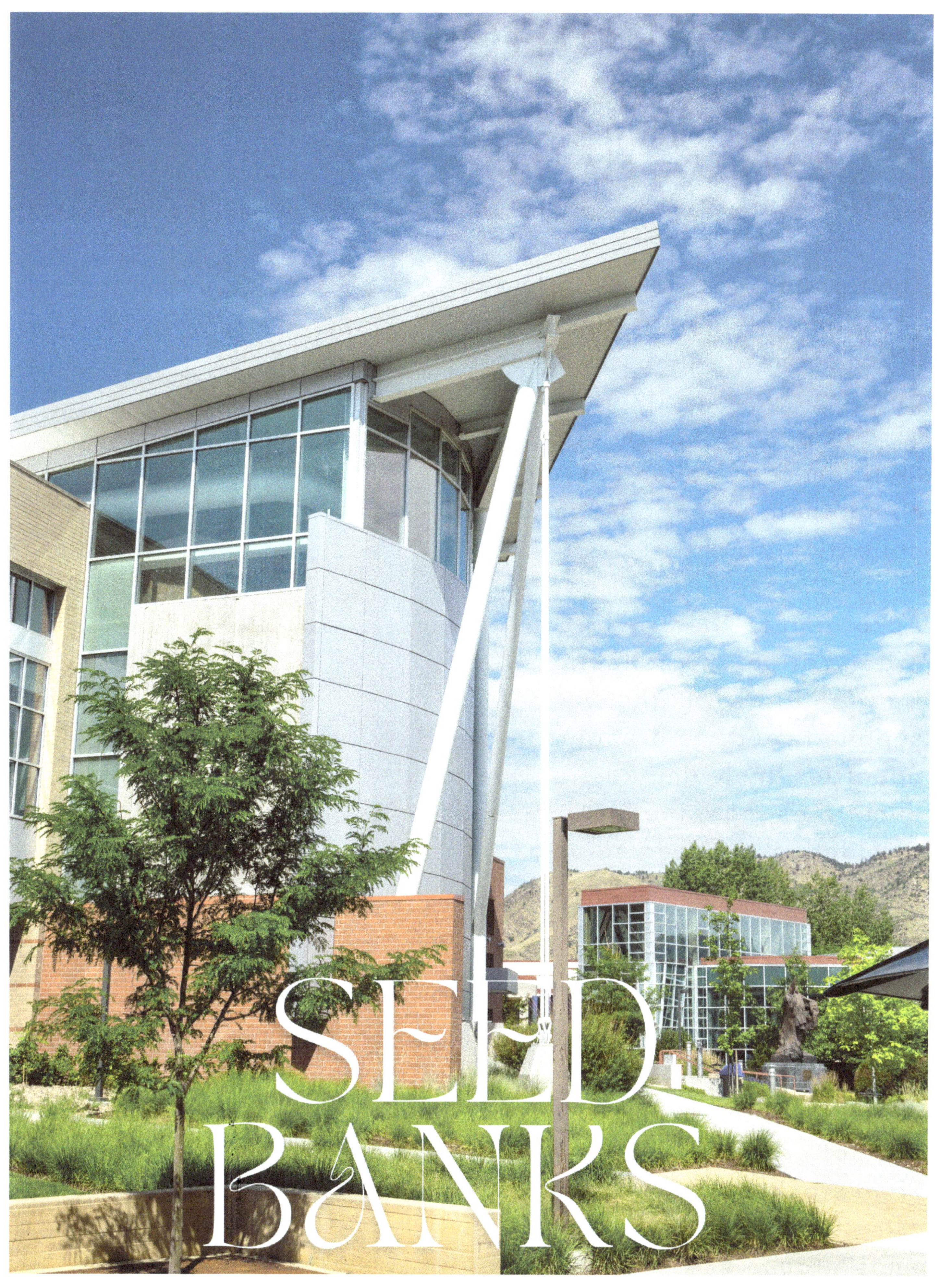

SEED
BANKS

the ukraine seed collection

The Spring of 2022 war between Ukraine and Russia brought about intense emotions. Russia ordered an attack on the city of Kharkiv, Ukraine's home to the largest heirloom seed collection and most comprehensive national seed bank collection.

According to the Crop Trust organization, the collection was the 10th largest in the world and supplied seeds to breeders in many countries, including Russia. Due to climate change, the historic seeds of elders are preserved as a legacy for today's farmers to rebuild with.

The National Gene Bank of Plants of Ukraine was bombed, losing over 160,000 seed samples saved as backups for emergencies. What did not perish was the majority of seed stock, preserved deep in a climate-controlled warehouse underground.∎

white earth land recovery

Winona LaDuke founded it in 1989, and its genesis was the 1986 federal White Earth Reservation Land Settlement Act (WELSA). The act cleared the land titles, and by 1989, after a series of litigation, closed the books on a settlement, Winona LaDuke and the White Earth Reservation of Ojibwe founded The White Earth Land Recovery Project.

The tribe worked together to grow and sell native wild rice, taking the funds and slowly buying back the land from willing participants.

By the early 1990s, the White Earth Land Project had repurchased over 1300 acres of reservation land. They tapped the sugar maples for syrup and grew beans, squash, tobacco, and heritage corn varieties.

In 2002, they added a 20-kilowatt wind turbine land built a seed bank, preserving heritage seeds. ∎

fort collins

Fort Collins is home to and known for craft beer. In fact, it is the craft beer capital of Colorado. How does that relate to seed banks and heirlooms? The craft beer and spirits industries are tied at the hip to grain growers for wheat, barley, and even hops, otherwise known as the "poor man's asparagus".

Seeds and commodities are the main ingredients when brewing and distilling. Seed banks may be even more important than the local ATM down the street.

Agricultural Genetic Resources Preservation Research: Fort Collins, CO, is located on the grounds of Colorado State University. The seed vault is home to almost 1 billion seed samples and over 150 livestock DNA samples.

The seed bank provides certification, education, outreach, crop, and soil sciences services. ∎

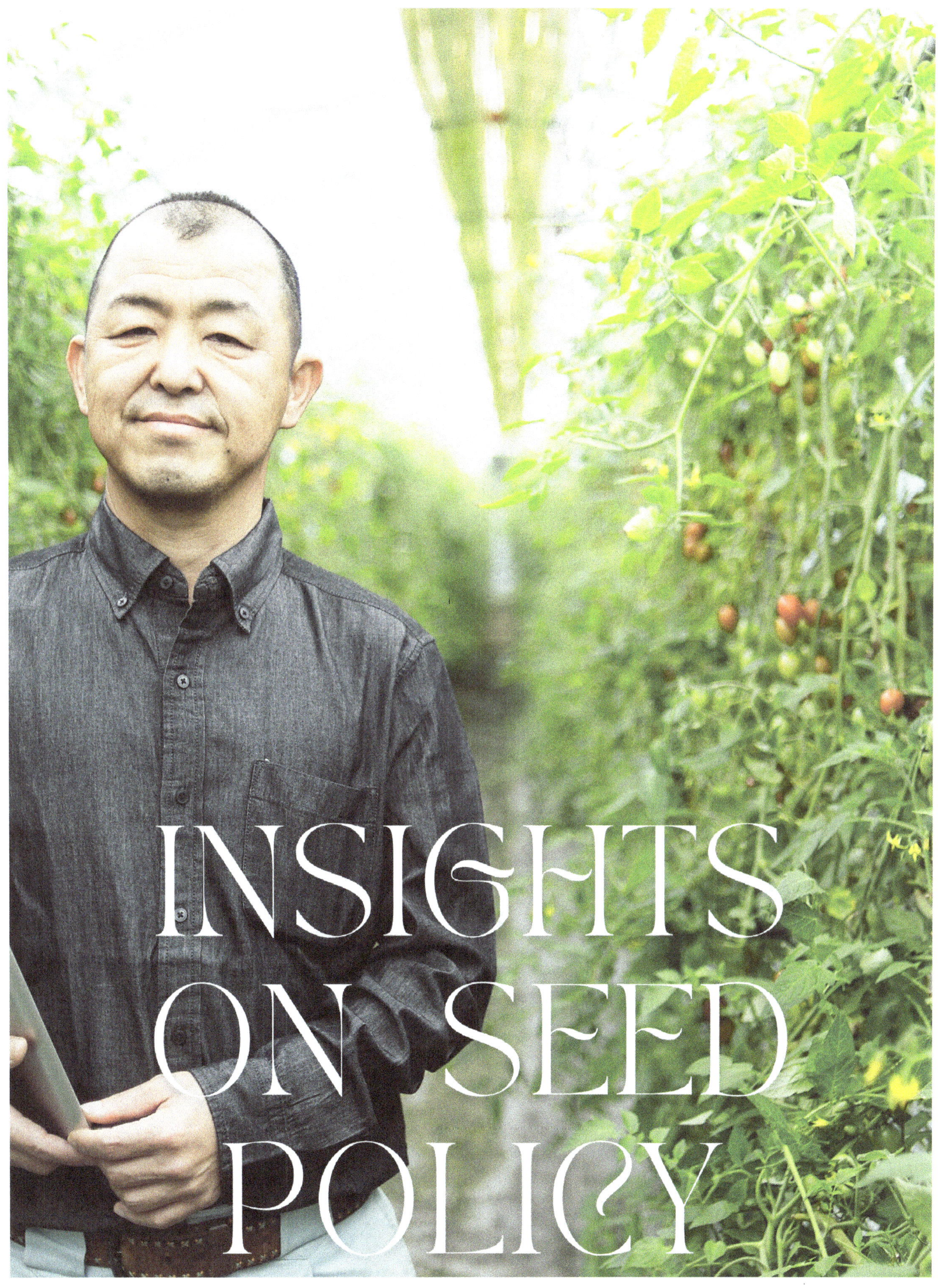
INSIGHTS
ON SEED
POLICY

beans

seed law

In 2018, Ursula Ramsey, now Assistant Professor of Business Law at the University of North Carolina Wilmington, authored The Georgetown Journal on Poverty Law and Policy Volume XXV, Number 2, titled Seed Libraries and Food Justice: Cultivating an Effective Legal and Policy Environment.

The article covered seed libraries, the legal landscape of the seed industry, healthy food policy, and recommendations for expanding seed libraries in the U.S.

The idea is to adopt a unifying law to create an exemption for non-commercial seed-sharing under each state's seed law.

The legal journal goes on to acknowledge the work being done by the Pennsylvania Department of Agriculture, which is issuing written guidance for seed librarians.

This guidance could act as a model for addressing heirloom seed

library statutes while raising awareness of how to set industry standards when working with uncharted territory.

Today, most farmers and gardeners cannot save or share patented and protected seeds, while breeders and small seed companies cannot use patented seeds to create new crop varieties.

It is important to understand three laws: The 1970 Plant Variety Protection Act (PVPA), The Federal Seed Act (FSA), and the U.S. Patent Law. Each intersects with seed usage, saving, and selling.

Organizations like [The Open Source Seed Initiative](), which models its movement after High-Tech open-source or free-like software practices, are building a system for small seed breeders to adopt practices similar to intellectual property (IP) rights and heirloom seed library laws.

This approach could ensure that some genes from seeds can be used to create new varieties or address climate-tolerant plants. ∎

REFERENCES

https://www.croptrust.org/work/svalbard-global-seed-vault

https://wellfieldgardens.org/2018/09/07/seed-storage

www.nrdc.org – National Resource Defense Council

https://www.seedsavers.org/

https://www.heifer.org/blog/how-to-save-your-seeds.htm

https://www.bhg.com/gardening/yard/garden-care/garden-seed-tips

https://wellfieldgardens.org/

https://extension.oregonstate.edu/

https://ucanr.edu/

https://seedalliance.org/

https://toxinfreeusa.org/

FURTHER READING

A Guide to Seed Intellectual Property Rights: https://seedalliance.org/publications/a-guide-to-seed-intellectual-property-rights/

Why Are Heirloom Seeds Illegal: https://storables.com/garden/when-did-gmo-seeds-start/

Heirloom: https://a.co/d/drWrEou

The Open Source Seed Initiative: https://osseeds.org/

ACKNOWLEDGEMENTS

I thank the farmers, seed companies, and historians for their support, encouragement, and inspiration. Thank you to the readers for taking the time to engage in these stories and for being inspired through my lens.

- Robin Bacon
@ForagingandFarming